D0315909

the ELF on the SHELF®

a Christmas tradition ™

SEARCH AND FIND

ORCHARD

ORCHARD BOOKS

First published in Great Britain in 2020 by The Watts Publishing Group

1 3 5 7 9 10 8 6 4 2

® and © 2020 CCA and B, LLC. All Rights Reserved.
Licensed by Rocket Licensing Ltd

Additional images © Shutterstock

Background illustrations © 2020 The Watts Publishing Group Limited

A CIP catalogue record for this book is available from the British Library

ISBN 978 1 40836 123 8

Printed and bound in China

MIX
Paper from
responsible sources
FSC
www.fsc.org
FSC® C104740

Orchard Books
An imprint of Hachette Children's Group
Part of The Watts Publishing Group Limited
Carmelite House
50 Victoria Embankment
London EC4Y 0DZ

An Hachette UK Company
www.hachette.co.uk
www.hachettechildrens.co.uk

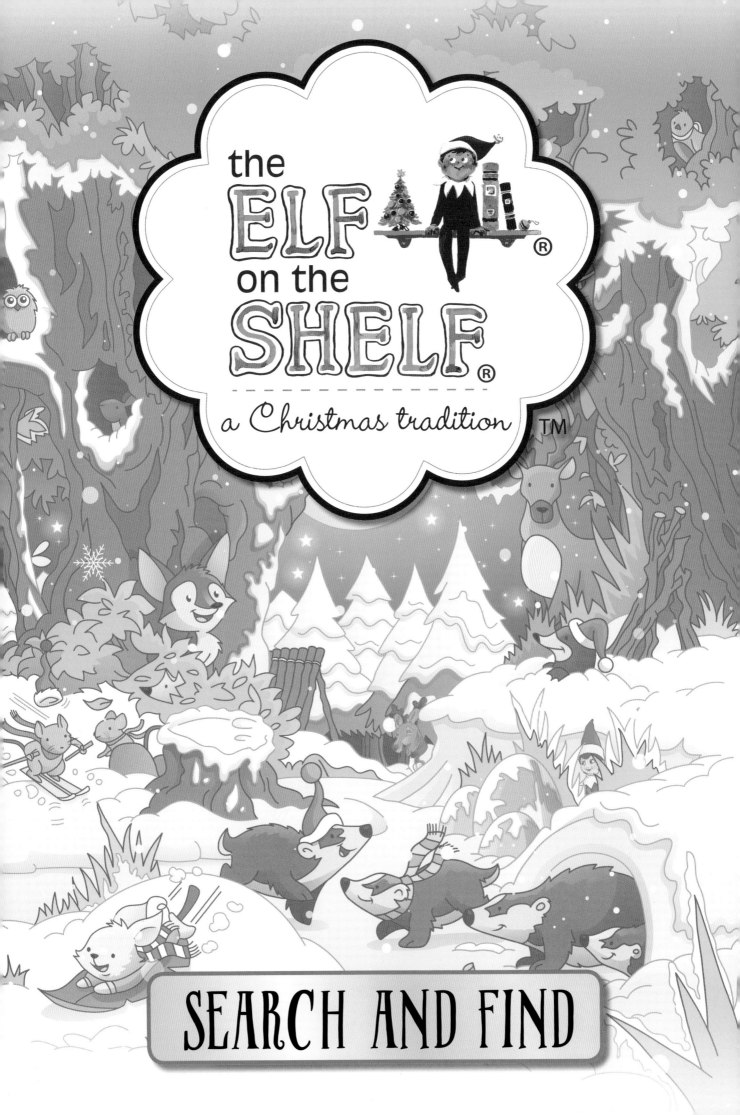

MEET THE SCOUT ELVES!

Welcome the Scout Elves and Elf Pets into the family by giving each one a name. Can you find each of them hiding on every page of this book?

MY NAME IS

sprout

MY NAME IS

lily

MY NAME IS

Snozeltrump

WINTER WONDERLAND

The weather is turning colder and the Scout Elves and Elf Pets are making their way to new homes. Can you find them travelling through the forest?

CHRISTMAS POST

All the children are sending Christmas cards to friends and family around the world. Can you spot the Scout Elves and Elf Pets hiding behind the stacks of letters?

Urgent Delivery

Have you ever seen so many letters? Spot the Scout Elves and Elf Pets hiding amongst them.

CHRISTMAS COOKING

It's busy in the kitchen as preparations for Christmas Day begin. The Scout Elves love making festive gingerbread. Can you spot the Scout Elves and Elf Pets in the scene?

CANDY CANES

The Scout Elves enjoy giving out Christmas sweets as much as they like eating them! Can you find the Scout Elves and Elf Pets among the candy canes?

CHRISTMAS MARKET

This market is full of Christmas cheer and merriment. See if you can spot the Scout Elves and Elf Pets among the shoppers.

A Helping Hand

Everyone in the factory has been building and fixing toys all year. Check out all the fun toys going to good girls and boys this Christmas. Can you find the silly Scout Elves and Elf Pets?

DECK THE HALLS

It's time to dress the tree ready for Christmas. Can you spot the Scout Elves and Elf Pets hiding among the ornaments?

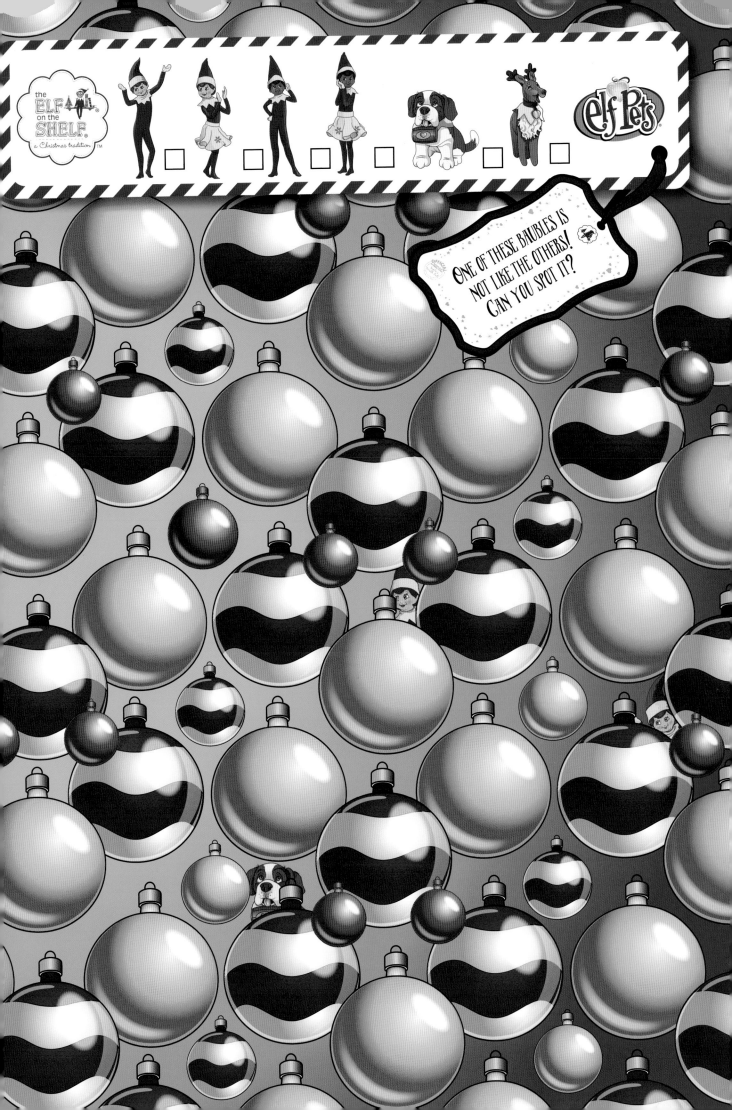

TOYS GALORE!

The Scout Elves are visiting the toy shop. Which toy would you choose? Can you spot the Scout Elves and Elf Pets hiding on the shop floor?

COSY CHRISTMAS EVE

It's Christmas Eve and the Scout Elves and Elf Pets are hiding out at home! Can you find them among the festive scene?

Elf Pets, Everywhere

So many Elf Pets! Will the Scout Elves be able to keep track of them all? Can you spot the Scout Elves hiding behind the Elf Pets?

CHRISTMAS FEAST

Everyone has gathered to share food, pull crackers and sing carols to celebrate the festive season. Can you spot the Scout Elves and Elf Pets having fun?

UNTIL NEXT YEAR!

Christmas is over and the Scout Elves and Elf Pets are enjoying a holiday. In this magical place the clouds are made of candy floss and everyone lives in waffle houses.

NAUGHTY OR NICE?

You made it onto the nice list. What would you like for Christmas? Find the Scout Elves and Elf Pets among the gifts.

ANSWERS

WINTER WONDERLAND

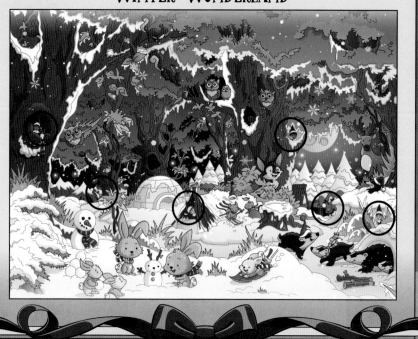

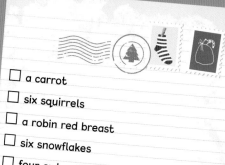

- a carrot
- six squirrels
- a robin red breast
- six snowflakes
- four owls
- a mole
- ten gold stars
- the moon
- two fallen branches
- two purple hats

CHRISTMAS POST

- ten gold stars
- a green helicopter
- nineteen white envelopes
- eighteen green boxes
- twelve red baubles
- two footballs
- a rubber stamp
- two sets of weighing scales
- an orange dinosaur
- ten green bows

Urgent Delivery

Christmas Cooking

- [ ] five wooden spoons
- [ ] four biscuit cutters
- [ ] fourteen wooden logs
- [ ] nine plates
- [ ] six mice
- [ ] an oven mitt
- [ ] a mouse hole
- [ ] two sugar shakers
- [ ] a green bottle
- [ ] two presents

CANDY CANES

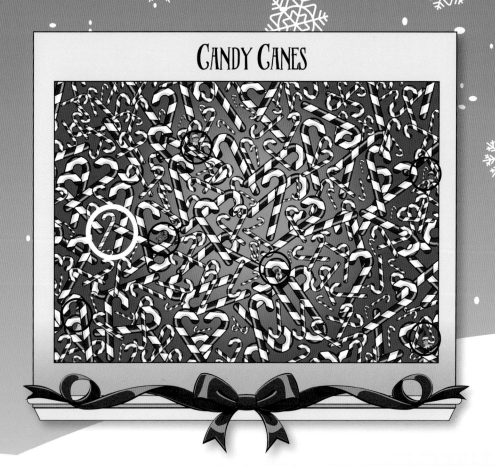

CHRISTMAS MARKET

- [ ] mistletoe
- [ ] eleven candy canes
- [ ] two hanging wreaths
- [ ] four green hats
- [ ] two people wearing antler headbands
- [ ] seven pretzels
- [ ] one bottle of mustard
- [ ] seven stockings
- [ ] eight mugs
- [ ] one pair of yellow wellies

A Helping Hand

- [ ] a hammer
- [ ] eleven rockets
- [ ] a toy car
- [ ] seven dolls
- [ ] a microphone
- [ ] five balls
- [ ] two trains
- [ ] four bicycles
- [ ] six animals wearing red and white hats
- [ ] a key

Deck the Halls

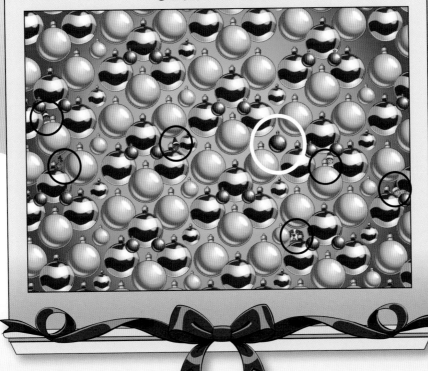

Toys Galore

- [ ] two spaceships
- [ ] eleven dinosaurs
- [ ] seven rockets
- [ ] two yo-yos
- [ ] four footballs
- [ ] four windmills
- [ ] two drums
- [ ] six building blocks
- [ ] three helicopters
- [ ] a games controller

- [ ] four mince pies
- [ ] nine greetings cards
- [ ] twelve candy canes
- [ ] five crackers
- [ ] a glass of milk
- [ ] two stockings
- [ ] three orange presents
- [ ] five blue baubles
- [ ] two pink flowers
- [ ] two yellow bows

Cosy Christmas Eve

ELF PETS EVERYWHERE

CHRISTMAS FEAST

- [ ] a mouse eating a sprout
- [ ] three Christmas trees
- [ ] seven paper crowns
- [ ] seven crackers
- [ ] four sprigs of holly
- [ ] thirteen presents
- [ ] twenty four carrots
- [ ] a pair of slippers
- [ ] a gingerbread person
- [ ] an umbrella

Until Next Year

- [ ] eight cherries
- [ ] seventeen flying sweets
- [ ] eight penguins
- [ ] four yellow eggs
- [ ] two chocolate bridges
- [ ] eight cupcakes
- [ ] twenty four lolly trees
- [ ] three waffle windows
- [ ] twenty candy canes
- [ ] six jelly beans

Naughty or Nice?